Believing God for Your Loved Ones

by
John Osteen

ISBN 0-912631-39-2

Believing God for Your Loved Ones

*And brought them out, and said, Sirs, what must I do to be saved? And they said, Believe on the Lord Jesus Christ, and **thou shalt be saved, and thy house*** (Acts 16:30,31).

Do you have sons, daughters, mothers, fathers, aunts and uncles, granddaddies, grandmothers, a mate—somebody in your family who needs to be saved? You must or you wouldn't be reading this booklet!

Did you know that because you are saved salvation is also available for your household? The Bible says, *Believe on the Lord Jesus Christ, and **thou shalt be saved, and thy house***. We can believe that God will touch our relatives and bring them into the Kingdom of God. We cannot just sit still and let our relatives in distant cities and other states and around the world be untouched by our concern. We may be

3

the only light they will ever have. And we must shine…we must reach out.

Maybe your relatives are somewhere in the darkness of sin. Many have been overcome by the powers of evil, wandering out in the highways and byways of life. It seems like they will never come home but I want you to know there is hope for them because YOU ARE THE KEY. You are the key for their salvation. You have a responsibility to them and God will use you if you are willing to die to yourself and pour out your life for them. One day you will rejoice because they'll come to God.

I had one relative who was deep in sin—away from God, away from the things of God. And for years I went along just doing nothing about it. Then one day while praying the Lord alerted me and said, "You'd better do something about that situation."

I began to reach out in love. I began to pray, "Satan, take your hands off my loved one. I bind you, Satan. I command you, demons, to get away from him in Jesus' Name. I surround him with God's love and mercy, wherever he is."

I prayed like that even though this person was hundreds and hundreds of miles away from me. You see, there's no distance in the spirit world. It's as though we're right there.

Daily I would pray for that loved one. I would say, as if that person were standing beside me, "Satan, I command you to take your hands off him. Demon powers, I rebuke you. I command you to leave his life. I break your power over his mind in Jesus' Name. I call him into the Kingdom of God. I surround him with love and mercy."

I did that every day. And I believed that Satan was leaving him, because he has to. The Bible says, *In my name shall they cast out devils* (Mark 16:17). God's power in the Name of Jesus drives the devil's power away. By faith, I would see light and grace and mercy surrounding him. Now, that happened whether I saw it in the natural or not because God said that we have the power to deliver others from the power of the enemy.

To make a long story short, that person began to take an interest in the things of God. Now, my relative has come to the Lord Jesus Christ—in full submission to His will—is saved and on his way to Heaven! God's Word works! We don't have to leave our family members in darkness!

But the urgency I have in my heart is this—don't go to sleep on the job. Don't say, "Well, they're not that close to me. They're a distant cousin, or an aunt or an uncle." Be serious about it—be concerned. And don't give up!

Remember, you have the Name that is above every name at your disposal (see Philippians 2:9-11). Just make up your mind, "I'm not going to let my son, my daughter, my mother or daddy, or any of my relatives go to hell. I'm going to reach out—I'm going to meet them in Heaven."

You can be the key for your loved ones to get to Heaven. Do everything you know to do—write a letter, make a telephone call, begin to pray, pray for them in the Holy Ghost, rebuke the devil—and God will see you through to victory.

The curse of the Law

Deuteronomy 28 shows us the curse of the Law and the blessing of the Law. Part of the curse has to do with our children. *Thy sons and thy daughters shall be given unto another people, and thine eyes shall look, and fail for longing for them all the day long: and there shall be no might in thine hand* (vs. 32). This verse is talking about our family circle. It says sons and daughters, but it could just as easily read aunts, uncles, mothers, and daddies.

The curse is to see your sons and daughters—your family members—go into the hands of the enemy. Who is our enemy? The Bible says, *Your adversary, the devil, as a roaring lion, walketh about, seeking whom he may devour* (1 Peter 5:7). What a tragedy to walk under the curse of the Law and see your family members in the hands of Satan, blinded and being pulled down to a devil's hell—and have no might in your hand, no power in your hand to help them. You see them in bondage to drugs, under the influence of alcohol, with broken homes, steeped in immorality, tormented in their minds, and there's nothing you can do to help them. That is the curse of the Law.

But I've got good news for you. Galatians 3:13,14 says, *Christ hath redeemed us from the curse of the law, being made a curse for us...that the blessing of Abraham might come on* [us].

The blessings are listed in the first 14 verses of Deuteronomy 28. If you belong to Jesus, *all these blessings shall come on thee, and overtake thee, if thou shalt hearken unto the voice of the Lord thy God. Blessed shalt thou be in the city, and blessed shalt thou be in the field. Blessed shall be the fruit of thy body* (vs. 2). God is concerned about our families. All our relatives can be saved and delivered and blessed. We need to reach out to those in need in our family circle.

Don't just say, "Well, somebody else will look after them." No. Just make up your mind that you are the one who can do something about it.

It's a terrible thing to be lost. What an awful thing to die without Jesus—to die without God. There is a hell. Jesus is the only way to Heaven. God has told us the truth in the Bible.

Oh, my, we need to witness to our mothers and daddies, our brothers and sisters! We need to compassionately love them and urge them to be saved and not be lost. Oh, the hour is so late, folks. We need to make up our mind that our families are going to be saved—that we're going to win them. We don't need them to join a church. They ought to go to church, but they need to join Jesus and let Him in their life.

My salvation experience

I remember when I first got saved. My brother had been saved and had gone into the Methodist ministry. He had a dramatic conversion that set him on fire for the Lord. He witnessed everywhere, to everyone. Through him I became awakened to the fact there was a God and that Jesus was the Savior. But I was so young that it really didn't have too much of an impact on me. Later, he went off to school and was gone for years while our family just stayed in town.

None of our family attended church regularly. Every once in a while we would go to some meeting. I remember one revival my mother took me to—it must have been a Holy Ghost meeting because the preacher nearly scared me to death. It was a tent meeting, and I never will forget the preacher's message. Someone had killed another person, then tied him to concrete and dumped him in the river. But somehow, the body had come loose, floated to the surface, and been found. This preacher screamed, "Be sure your sins will find you out," and my hair stood up on end! I remember it as if it happened yesterday.

And then I can remember going to church and standing beside Mother, singing, "This is my story, this is my song—praising my Savior all the day long." I know I went to Sunday school once or twice, but outside of that I wasn't exposed to much spiritual influence.

But I thank God for a young man named Sam Martin, who began to witness to me. I wasn't even his relative, but he began to tell me about Jesus. He planted a seed in my heart about God.

He didn't talk to me about church, the Bible, or the Holy Ghost. He told me how to be saved. He didn't argue doctrine with me. He wasn't ashamed of the Lord Jesus Christ.

In high school, when we had to give reports, he'd give a report on Jesus. He'd stand up boldly for the Lord Jesus Christ. And he'd always tell me, "John, you ought to be saved." I was ashamed that I knew him. I'd go across the street to keep from walking close to him because he was so outlandish with his talking about Jesus.

I remember coming home from a nightclub in south Ft. Worth, Texas, lost and and undone without

God. Oh, I had a desire for God but I was afraid to commit my life to Him. But He began to stir my heart. The Father began to draw me. Jesus said, "No man can come to Me except the Father draw him" (see John 6:44). I knew I needed God, but I was afraid of Him. I was afraid to commit myself to the Lord.

I got home at two o'clock in the morning and looked around for a Bible. I looked all over the house but couldn't find one. Finally, I found the old family Bible—the huge kind with all the family records in it. I sat down at the dining room table in the early morning hours, as a lost young man, seeking the Lord, trying to find peace in my heart—afraid of God. And I read, and read, and read, and you know, I couldn't understand one single solitary thing I read. The Bible says, *The natural man receiveth not the things of the Spirit of God...neither can he know them, because they are spiritually discerned* (1 Corinthians 2:14).

So I closed that Bible—I never will forget this...it's as real as if it happened yesterday—and went to the screen door to go outside. And just as my hand touched the screen door—something, or rather, "Somebody" said, "Go back and open the Bible." Thank God, I had enough sense to do that. I went back to the table and just casually flipped open the Bible. It opened at a great big beautiful picture of Jesus, standing at a door and knocking. And underneath it said, *Behold, I stand at the door, and knock: if any man*—well, that included me—*hear my voice, and open the door, I will come in to him* (Revelation 3:20). I looked at that picture and thought, *Behold, I stand at the door and knock. Now, that must mean my heart's door—that God is trying to knock on my heart.*

Then I grabbed a quilt and went outside to lie down on the grass. I looked up at the stars in their stately march across the heavens and I thought, *Oh, God, what will I do when I die? What's going to happen to me when I grow older and go out into eternity?*

I lay there on that pallet that night and thought about God—and I thought about Sam Martin. I remembered him telling me about God.

So I called him on the phone the next day and said, "Sam, I had a strange thing happen to me coming home from the nightclub last night." And I told him about the picture and the stars and thinking about God. What's wrong with me?"

"Why, John," Sam answered, "you're under the conviction of sin." And I thought, *Dear God, what's that?* I didn't know what any of these religious terms meant.

"Sam," I said, "I want to go to church with you." I'd promised to go to church with him many times but always backed out. So we arranged a time and date.

And I want you to know I beat him there that Sunday morning. I never will forget it—I saw his pickup truck coming around the corner and he was looking for me like an eagle looking for a sparrow! We went into the church and sat down. I don't remember what the minister preached. I could have cared less—I just wanted to get down the aisle.

When the time came for the invitation, it just seemed like the devil nailed my shoes to the floor—I couldn't move. I couldn't do anything. Finally, Sam put his arm around me and said, "John, I'll go with you if you'll go."

I never will forget that trek. Oh, I didn't know much about this great Heavenly Father, but I knew my heart was empty and the world couldn't satisfy me. So I stood up, looked at Sam, and walked down that aisle to the front of the church. The preacher took my hand and said, "Do you take Jesus as your Lord?"

I said, "I don't know—I'm a wicked man. I'm a sinner."

He smiled and said, "I didn't ask you that—will you take Jesus as your Lord and Savior?"

I never will forget what I said next. "Absolutely." When I said that, I passed out of darkness into light, from death to life. What a glorious day that was! I was so thrilled to be saved, to know Jesus.

On the way home, I passed a Gulf gas station and went into the rest room and got down on my knees and prayed. Isn't that something! I didn't get the baptism in the Holy Ghost until 19 years later, but I got saved and became a preacher of the Gospel.

In fact, three weeks after I got saved I was preaching! Six weeks after I got saved, I was preaching three times a week. You say, "Where were you preaching? Who invited you?" Nobody invited me. I just went.

I went to the jails and to the streets. I went to the rest homes—they called them poor farms then. And I went to the missions. God just put it in my heart that He had called me to preach. I couldn't believe it at first. To be saved is glorious enough, but it was hard for me to comprehend that He would call me to preach!

My first convert

My whole family used to go to nightclubs. They didn't care anything about God. I usually went with them, but now that I was saved, I didn't go.

Day after day went by and I didn't go with them. One time when supper was over and the dishes were cleaned off, I went and hauled out that great big old Bible—the only one I had—and put it down on the table to read it. I didn't understand a whole lot then, but I began to understand a little bit. My family just left me alone like a ghost was in the house.

Then one night, my sister Mary saw me at my usual post at the table. She was going out to a nightclub like the rest of the family but she came in and stood by my side. She stood there for a moment and then asked, "John, why do you stay here and not go with us anymore? Why do you stay here and read the Bible? Why are you doing this?"

I figured it was time for me to say something because I hadn't said anything to anybody yet. They just knew that I didn't do what I used to do, and had started reading the Bible. So I looked at her and cautiously said, "Mary, I've let Jesus into my heart. He's become my Lord and Savior and I'm through living for the world." Then I looked back down at that old Bible. I was afraid she was going to jump down my throat. When I looked back at her, tears were running down her face.

"John, do you think Jesus would save anybody like me?" she asked.

And I said, "Yes, I think He would." And I led my sister Mary to the Lord. She knelt right there and gave her heart to Jesus.

A friend gets saved

Then I tried to talk to one of my good buddies that I'd "painted the town red" with so many times. I was afraid to talk to him at first because I knew he was "wild and woolly." But I was really afraid to tell him I'd given my heart to Jesus.

He asked me to go out with him one Saturday night after I got saved. And I said, "No, Ben, I'm not going to go out."

"Why not?" he asked. "We go out every Saturday night. You know what we do."

"I'm not going to do it anymore," I replied rather timidly.

"Yes, you are," he laughed. "You're going to go with me."

"No, I'm not going to do it," I said, looking him square in the eye this time.

He looked at me and laughed even harder. "I know what's happened to you—you've become one of those Christians."

And when he laughed, something rose up in me. "Yes, I have. And I'm not going with you anymore. I'm on the trail with Jesus!" And I spun around on my heels and left.

Then he started following me around. He used to come down to the theater where I worked and walk me home. Every once in a while he'd try to talk to me about God. He'd walk beside me and ask, "Are you going to church?" And I'd say, "Yeah." And we'd just keep on walking.

Then he'd ask, "Well, what happens there?" And I'd tell him, "We have church."

Every day we would walk home together and cut through a vacant lot into a back alley behind his garage. When we got to his house, we'd part company and I'd walk the rest of the way home by myself. But this particular day he stopped—right behind his garage. I can still see him in my mind's eye. He wore a hat and a zoot-suit. He stood there, looking at me, and said, almost defiantly, "John Osteen, I'm not moving. I know you've got something I want. I don't know what it is and you won't tell me, but I'm not moving from behind this garage until you tell me how to get it!"

"Ben, I don't know exactly how to tell you. All I know is, I was a sinner and needed to accept Jesus Christ as my Lord and Savior. And God saved me."

Then, in one swift move, he took off his hat, knelt down, and said, "Then I'm going to let Him do that to me, too." So I knelt down beside him and we prayed together.

Years later, Ben became a high-ranking Air Force officer at the Pentagon. We would visit together when he'd come home, and every time he'd say, "John, let's go by that old place and look. That's where I knelt—right there—that's where I found the Lord." And then we'd just have a glorious time praising the Lord.

Daddy gets saved

Soon after that I began to reach out to other members of my family.

14

My daddy never did take us to church. I do not ever remember my daddy taking me to church, even once. My mother took me a few times. That is a sad thing. I do not say that in any derogatory sense but it is just the truth. My father did not know God. He never talked to us about God. He was good to us, a good father, but he never talked to us about God. He never knew the Lord Jesus Christ. When I got saved, when I gave my heart to Jesus, I knew my daddy was lost and was going to go to hell. I knew he would not be interested in God on his own so I decided that I was going to pray for his salvation. I was determined to win him to the Lord. I even put the devil on notice. I said, "Devil, you are not going to have my daddy."

Oh, I loved my daddy. One thing I liked about him was that he was shorter than I am. He was a little Dutchman about five foot five. He was a precious person, but lost.

Daddy didn't know much about God or eternity. He would say, "John, when I'm dead, I'm dead like a dog. Just roll me over in the ditch. There is nothing after this life." He really believed that.

I said, "Daddy, if there is nothing after death, if you do not exist anymore and you die like a dog to be rolled over in the ditch, I would forget my concern about you. If that was true, I would never bother you again.

"But Daddy," I pleaded, "it's just not true. The eternal Word of God declares that you are made in the image of God. You have to live somewhere. There are only two places to go—Heaven or hell. Without Jesus you will die and go to hell.

"I am not going to give up. I am going to stand for you, Daddy. I am going to go before God and believe for your salvation."

Mother had given herself to the Lord, but we really had our work cut out for us with Daddy. I continued to talk to him about being saved and he would say, "No, I'm all right. I'm just as good as some of those hypocrites in the church."

If some of your unsaved family members or friends have said that, you might remind them of this: If you're hiding behind a hypocrite, you're littler than they are. And if you don't like them here, you'd better make sure you go to Heaven, because if you don't, you'll be penned up in hell with all the hypocrites for the rest of eternity!

Once I held a revival in Dallas in a Baptist church and I asked Mother to bring Daddy to the meetings. Now my mother had strong faith, so she secretly put some extra clothes in the car thoroughly expecting him to be saved and baptized during the revival.

I preached Friday night and Saturday night and Daddy didn't make a move. But on Sunday morning while I was preaching my sermon, he got up out of his seat, walked down the aisle and right up on the platform with me. He stood next to me and said, "I'm going to finish today what I started 20-25 years ago. I'm giving my heart to the Lord Jesus Christ."

I asked Daddy later what he meant by "finishing what he had started" and he said, "Years ago, I got lost in the fields during a snowstorm. I was about to pass out from the cold. I was numb and knew I was going to freeze to death. I couldn't move and I cried out to God, 'God, if You'll get me out of this, I'll serve You.' I woke up later as warm as toast. God spared my life and I forgot my promise." Nobody knew about Daddy's vow, but God did. And Daddy never forgot it.

Oh, let's shake ourselves. God said that we can be saved...*and our household!* Write a letter, make a telephone call, go see your loved ones and give your testimony, go share the love of God, do something about it. Don't let time get away from you. Reach out to your relatives and command the devil to leave them. Daily, in your prayer time, surround them with love and mercy and call them into the Kingdom of God. Romans 2:4 says that the goodness of God leads people to repentance. Believe God that they'll be saved and meet you in Heaven.

Don't give up! Don't have any quittin' sense— just keep on. One day they'll come up to you in Heaven and say, "Thank God, you didn't give up on me. Thank God, you witnessed to me. Thank God, I found the Lord because you wouldn't give up. I cursed you. I told you to get away. I told you I wasn't interested, but you wouldn't give up on me. Thank God, I'm in Heaven because of you." Wouldn't that be a joyous thing?

A lamb for a house

Some of you may be thinking, "Yes, but do I have any Scripture in the Bible to believe in—to cling to and remind God of—to claim and believe that every one of my children, my husband, or my wife will not be lost, that they'll be saved? Is there any way that I can claim my household? Oh, it would be a terrible thing to be taken out of the world early and leave your children or husband or wife here in this dark world, lost and undone. How will they ever find salvation? Will somebody ever tell them about Jesus?

The Old Testament tells how God sent judgment against the land of Egypt when Pharaoh refused to obey God's command to release the Israelites from captivity. Because of his disobedience, God sent a plague to smite all the firstborn children in Egypt.

To protect the Israelites from this plague, God instructed them to sacrifice "a lamb for a house." The blood of a sacrificed lamb was to be applied to the doorposts of each Jewish home. God said when He saw the Lamb's blood, He would "pass over" them and the plague would not destroy the members of that household. The blood of that sacrificial lamb was what saved the family members.

The Bible says in Exodus 12:3 that we are to take a "lamb for a house." Who is that Lamb? When John the Baptist said, "Behold the Lamb of God that taketh away the sin of the world," who was he talking about? Jesus! Jesus is the Lamb we are to cling to for our household. You can take the Lamb of God for your whole house.

Does that mean your child can never be lost? No—a thousand times no. Does it assure you that your child can never ever be anything but saved? No. But it is a promise. It is a declaration, and if you will claim it, if you will hold onto it, daring to remind God of it—if you will climb the celestial stairway to where the blood has been sprinkled in the heavenlies and say, "Father, You said I could have a lamb for my house. Jesus is that Lamb. I take the Lamb for my children, my husband, my wife, my whole house I claim for God"—God will hear your prayer.

I believe the Jesus who wept over Jerusalem knows that we cannot be happy without knowing that somehow we can claim our families. And that's why I think He wrote indelibly upon the pages of holy writ that there can be a lamb for a house. And no matter how far that son or daughter wanders in sin, how dark their lives may be, there can be a mother or a daddy who will hold onto God and say, "A lamb for a house." And God will act.

Claiming a lamb for your family

There is a man in my church whose mother worried and worried about her son because he did not live for God. Did that mother give up? No, she claimed the promise of God and took a lamb for her house.

She held that promise up to God and said, "No matter what it takes, God, bring him to You." This is how we ought to pray. "Whatever it takes, may the Lamb of God bring my children, my mother, my daddy, my husband, my wife, my household to God. I claim them for my God." Today that man is serving the Lord—all because his mother claimed a lamb for her house.

You remind Jesus of your family—take your family to God. I don't know what you do as a parent, but many times when my children were living at home, I would go into their rooms at night while they were sleeping and pray that God's precious Holy Spirit and His angels would linger near them, that God would speak to them and continue to keep them from the evil of the world. I'm grateful my children do not desire the world—they're good children.

It delights the heart of a parent to go where your children sleep and pray and take a lamb for your household. Don't doubt God when you take your children to God. Don't let the devil fill your heart with fear. There's no devil in or out of hell that can rob one of your children. They will serve God because you have taken a lamb for your household. Claim God's promises and hold on to them—don't doubt, don't waver—climb up to God where the sprinkled blood of the Lamb of God has been applied to the mercy seat and say, "Father, I take that Lamb—Your Son—not only for myself, but for my household." And the God who made the worlds will begin to act, He will begin to move in the behalf of your children.

Your children may be old, or perhaps communication has broken down between you and you don't know where they are. But God knows. And He'll do whatever it takes to bring them to himself if you'll take a lamb for your house, claim the promises of God, and believe and have faith in Him.

An entire family saved

One time I was in the hospital for some tests and had the opportunity to witness to a man that was going to have open heart surgery. He broke down and cried when I told him of Jesus' wonderful love for him. Then we prayed together for him to receive Jesus as his Lord and Savior.

Later, that afternoon, he came back to my hospital room with his wife. She, too, was gloriously saved.

The next day, the day before his surgery, he came back again with his older daughter. I asked her, "Do you know Jesus?" And she quickly answered, "Oh, yes. But nearly all our family is down in Dad's room and we want you to come and talk to them. Not all of them are Christians." You see, God wants a lamb for a house. I said, "You go on back, I'll be down there in a little bit."

After a while I went down to see that man—his room was packed full of children and in-laws. I closed the door behind me and began to tell them how the Lord saved me.

Then I looked each one of them in the eye and asked, "Do you know the Lord? Are you really saved?" Three or four didn't know the Lord. And so I began to tell them how to be saved.

One by one, with tears running down their eyes, they accepted Jesus as their Savior. And then, as they sat in that holy moment, we began to sing, "Amazing grace, how sweet the sound, That saved a wretch like me! I once was lost, but now am found—was blind, but now I see." Oh, Jesus was so real!

About the time we started singing, the door opened and the oldest son—a great big, strong, husky fellow—came in with his wife and teen-aged daughter. And as I looked at them, the devil whispered in my ear, "Leave him alone—it's all over. You don't need to go through all this with him." But Jesus said, "No, don't leave him out." So I told him briefly what we were doing and why we were singing.

I turned to his wife and asked, "Are you a Christian?"

And she answered, "Oh, yes, I know Jesus."

Next I asked his teen-aged daughter, "Are you a Christian?"

And she replied, "Oh, yes, I know Jesus."

Then I looked that big strong man square in the eye and asked, "Do you know the Lord?"

"No," he answered. "I'm lost. I'm not a Christian."

"Jesus has dealt with your heart many times, hasn't He?"

"Oh, yes."

"Wouldn't you like to open your heart, as these have, and give your heart to Jesus?" I asked him.

He clasped my hand, burst into tears, and said, "Yes, oh, yes, I want to be saved." And then the circle was completed. Jesus blessed that family by saving every one of them.

Rescue your family

Folks, we cannot take our families for granted. We must claim a lamb for our family. We must believe that wherever they are—no matter what hell hole they may be in—that we can claim them for God. God will not forget a mother or a father's prayers and those prayers will follow their children—somewhere along life's road, God is going to answer those prayers. The God who cannot lie will never let them go.

There's an old song that says, "There were ninety and nine that safely lay in the shelter of the fold. But one was out on the hills away, far off from the gates of gold...And all through the mountains, thunder riven, and up from the rocky steep, there arose a glad cry to the gates of heaven, 'Rejoice, I have found My sheep!'"

God will seek your son, your daughter, your mother, your father, your husband, your wife. He'll go through the mountains, He'll go through the valleys. He'll answer your prayer. He cannot go back on His promise.

Take a lamb for your household. Claim your children, your family members for God. Don't give your son, your daughter, your family over to the devil. Don't do it. Climb beyond the stars and march down through the gates of pearl, down the streets of gold, beside the glorious stream, and daily go before the throne of God. Say, "The Lamb of God is for my household—for my husband, my wife, my children. Wherever they are, oh, God, arrest them. Whatever it takes, bring them in."

Sometimes we say, "My daughter is too bad, my son is too bad. My daddy is too far gone on his way to hell. My relative is too strung out on drugs—it's too late." But with Jesus, it's never too late! Second Peter 3:9 says that God is not willing that any man or woman perish, but that *all* should come to repentance. IT'S NEVER TOO LATE!

You may ask, "Will God hear the prayer of the sinner?" Sure, God will hear a sinner pray. That's the way He heard me pray when I asked Him to save me.

We need to be stirred up enough to say, "No! I'm not going to let the devil have my son. I'm not going to let the devil have my daughter. I'm not going to let the devil have my wife. I'm not going to let the devil have my husband."

Oh, my friend, don't give up! Don't give up. *YOU ARE THE KEY FOR SOMEBODY*. You can rescue your family members. Take them back from the enemy. Don't let the devil have them!

I do not know about you, but I am determined that I am going to be the key to my family and many others. I am not going to let them go to hell.

You've got to get concerned about your relatives—I'm not just talking about feeling a little concern— you've got to cry out to God for them. I'm talking about intercession—someone to cry out for those who are not right with God. In the Amplified Bible, Job 22:30 says, *He will deliver those for whom you intercede although they are not innocent*. Only the guilty need mercy!

Are you going to leave demon powers ravaging your mate, your child, your relative, your friend? You may be the only person who will ever pray, the only person who will ever care. Oh, stir yourself up! Draw nigh to God. Don't give up! Don't leave them to the demon powers.

Untold legions—millions of demons—have been unleashed on our generation. No other generation has ever been so subjected to the evil control of drugs and alcohol ruining the minds and futures of people. Many of our relatives have fallen victim to this diabolical plot. It seems the devil is taking over. Is there an answer?

The world tells people to go to this doctor or that doctor; take this pill or that pill. We ought to be telling them about the only pill to take—the "gos-pill"! Jesus said in the Great Commission, *These signs shall follow them that believe* (Mark 16:17). And the first sign to follow the believer is, *In my name shall they cast out devils* (vs. 17). He didn't say to beg them to go out, or invite them to go out. He said, *I give unto you power to tread on serpents and scorpions, and over all the power of the enemy* (Luke 10:19). You're supposed to cast out demons in the Name of Jesus!

We ought to rise up and use the power of Jesus' Name to drive the devil from our homes, our children, our relatives.

The devil doesn't care how many college degrees you have. I'm an ordained minister, but devils have never asked me if I was ordained. I have a bachelor's degree, a master's degree, and two doctor's degrees, but no demon has ever asked me about those degrees. All he asks me is, "What Name are you coming in?" And I say, "In the Name of Jesus." And that's what gets the job done.

Is the devil destroying your daddy? Is he destroying your mother? Is the devil destroying your mate? Is he destroying your aunt, your uncle, your son, your daughter? Well, you can do something about it. You can use the Name of Jesus to drive the devil out.

With patience we inherit the promises

Have you ever prayed and it seemed like God went on the other side of heaven, sat down, and ignored you? Well, that does not mean God doesn't love you. Just because you have not had an answer yet, does not mean you are not going to get an answer.

Mothers, Dads, listen to me. Don't you give up on your son or daughter. Husbands and wives, don't give up on your mates. You might not have heard from heaven yet, but God will answer your prayer. The Bible says, *Through faith and patience* [we] *inherit the promises* (Hebrews 6:12). So claim the lamb for your household. Hold fast. Having done all…stand. Keep standing. **Do not be moved!**

YOU ARE THE KEY TO SOMEONE! Do not give up. You are the only hope. You are the only light. You are the only person. Do not give up on that mate, that daddy, that mother, that boy, or that girl. It does not matter how far down the road they have gone. If you will go before God and stand for them and not give up, the God of Heaven who answers prayer will begin to work in their behalf and one day, you will see them delivered from the power of the devil and set free!

If you have a relative who needs God, you can stand in the gap for them, interceding for them before the throne of God. God is looking for someone to stand in the gap for the lost. See Psalm 106:23, *Amplified Version* and Ezekiel 22:30.

Say this out loud: **"Oh, God, I want my relatives to be delivered from the devil and demon powers. Lord, I come to You in the behalf of my loved ones, my relatives, and I am believing they will be delivered, set free, washed, cleansed, forgiven, saved, and will go to Heaven. I believe that in my heart and I speak it out of my mouth, in Jesus' Name."**

Now clench your fist and say:

"Devil, demons, in Jesus' Name I command you to take your hands off my relatives. In the Name of Jesus, I won't let you have them. They're going to go to Heaven, they're not going to hell. They're going to have joy here on earth and not hell on earth. I claim them and I command you to leave them in Jesus' Name. I break your power

over their mind, their body, and their spirit. I set them free.

"I'll do my part, Father, to bring them to know Jesus. Thank You, Father, they're surrounded with love and mercy and Your goodness. I claim them for the Kingdom of God, in Jesus' Name. Amen."

Your loved ones are going to come to Jesus. They are going to be set free from the power of the devil and serve God the rest of their lives.

Some of you have no one to be a key. There is not a friend, a mother, a daddy who cares. That touches my heart. There are thousands upon thousands of people who have no one—no one cares. There is not a person praying that you can think of—not one relative who knows God. I hear your cries saying, "Nobody cares for me. I am tormented. I am lost and nobody cares. I have no one."

But I have news for you today. I will be that someone. I want you to know God loves you—no matter how you have lived in the past. You can accept Jesus as your Lord and Savior today. I want you to pray this prayer with me: **"Oh, God, I know without Jesus I am lost. I know without Jesus that I will die and go to hell. But God, I don't want to be lost. I want to be saved. I turn away from the devil and my old way of living. I will never go that way again. I turn to You, Jesus, and I ask You to come into my heart. Be my Lord and Savior. God, You are now more than my God. You are my Heavenly Father and I am Your child. I am in the family of God. Thank You, Jesus for saving me. Amen."**

We are going to the Father for you. Where nobody else cares, we care. We are going to believe God for you. If you have been saved through reading this booklet, write and tell us. We want to rejoice with you. God bless you!

JOHN OSTEEN MINISTRIES
ORDER FORM

QTY	DESCRIPTION	PRICE EACH	TOTAL
	A MIRACLE FOR YOUR MARRIAGE	$1.25	
	A PLACE CALLED THERE	$ .75	
	ABC'S OF FAITH	.75	
	BELIEVING GOD FOR YOUR LOVED ONES	$1.25	
	DECEPTION! RECOGNIZING TRUE AND FALSE MINISTRIES	.75	
	FOUR PRINCIPLES IN RECEIVING FROM GOD	.75	
	HOW TO CLAIM THE BENEFITS OF THE WILL*	1.25	
	HOW TO DEMONSTRATE SATAN'S DEFEAT	1.25	
	HOW TO FLOW IN THE SUPER SUPERNATURAL	1.50	
	HOW TO MINISTER HEALING TO THE SICK	.75	
	HOW TO RECEIVE LIFE ETERNAL*	.75	
	HOW TO RELEASE THE POWER OF GOD	1.50	
	KEEP WHAT GOD GIVES	.75	
	LOVE & MARRIAGE	.75	
	OVERCOMING HINDRANCES TO RECEIVING THE BAPTISM IN THE HOLY SPIRIT	2.00	
	PULLING DOWN STRONGHOLDS*	1.25	
	RECEIVE THE HOLY SPIRIT*	.75	
	REIGNING IN LIFE AS A KING	5.00	
	RIVERS OF LIVING WATER	1.75	
	SATURDAY'S COMING	.75	
	THE BELIEVER'S #1 NEED	1.25	
	THE BIBLE WAY TO SPIRITUAL POWER	1.50	

*AVAILABLE IN SPANISH

SUBTOTAL A

ORDER FORM CONTINUED NEXT PAGE.

QTY	DESCRIPTION	PRICE EACH	TOTAL
	THE CONFESSIONS OF A BAPTIST PREACHER	5.00	
	THE DIVINE FLOW*	1.25	
	THE 6TH SENSE...FAITH*	1.25	
	THE TRUTH SHALL SET YOU FREE	1.25	
	THERE IS A MIRACLE IN YOUR MOUTH*	1.25	
	THIS AWAKENING GENERATION	1.75	
	UNRAVELING THE MYSTERY OF THE BLOOD COVENANT	2.50	
	WHAT TO DO WHEN NOTHING SEEMS TO WORK*	.75	
	WHAT TO DO WHEN THE TEMPTER COMES	1.25	
	YOU CAN CHANGE YOUR DESTINY	1.50	

*AVAILABLE IN SPANISH

SUBTOTAL A	
SUBTOTAL B	
POSTAGE & HANDLING	$1.00
TOTAL AMOUNT ENCLOSED	

NAME _____

ADDRESS _____

CITY _____ STATE _____ ZIP _____

WRITE FOR A COMPLETE LIST OF JOHN OSTEEN'S TEACHING MATERIALS IN THE JOHN OSTEEN FAITH LIBRARY CATALOGUE. MANNA MAGAZINE IS AVAILABLE UPON REQUEST FREE AND POSTAGE PAID. WRITE TO:

JOHN OSTEEN MINISTRIES
P.O. BOX 23117
HOUSTON, TEXAS 77228

JOHN OSTEEN MINISTRIES
ORDER FORM

QTY	DESCRIPTION	PRICE EACH	TOTAL
	A MIRACLE FOR YOUR MARRIAGE	$1.25	
	A PLACE CALLED THERE	$ .75	
	ABC'S OF FAITH	.75	
	BELIEVING GOD FOR YOUR LOVED ONES	$1.25	
	DECEPTION! RECOGNIZING TRUE AND FALSE MINISTRIES	.75	
	FOUR PRINCIPLES IN RECEIVING FROM GOD	.75	
	HOW TO CLAIM THE BENEFITS OF THE WILL*	1.25	
	HOW TO DEMONSTRATE SATAN'S DEFEAT	1.25	
	HOW TO FLOW IN THE SUPER SUPERNATURAL	1.50	
	HOW TO MINISTER HEALING TO THE SICK	.75	
	HOW TO RECEIVE LIFE ETERNAL*	.75	
	HOW TO RELEASE THE POWER OF GOD	1.50	
	KEEP WHAT GOD GIVES	.75	
	LOVE & MARRIAGE	.75	
	OVERCOMING HINDRANCES TO RECEIVING THE BAPTISM IN THE HOLY SPIRIT	2.00	
	PULLING DOWN STRONGHOLDS*	1.25	
	RECEIVE THE HOLY SPIRIT*	.75	
	REIGNING IN LIFE AS A KING	5.00	
	RIVERS OF LIVING WATER	1.75	
	SATURDAY'S COMING	.75	
	THE BELIEVER'S #1 NEED	1.25	
	THE BIBLE WAY TO SPIRITUAL POWER	1.50	

*AVAILABLE IN SPANISH

SUBTOTAL A

ORDER FORM CONTINUED NEXT PAGE.

QTY	DESCRIPTION	PRICE EACH	TOTAL
	THE CONFESSIONS OF A BAPTIST PREACHER	5.00	
	THE DIVINE FLOW*	1.25	
	THE 6TH SENSE...FAITH*	1.25	
	THE TRUTH SHALL SET YOU FREE	1.25	
	THERE IS A MIRACLE IN YOUR MOUTH*	1.25	
	THIS AWAKENING GENERATION	1.75	
	UNRAVELING THE MYSTERY OF THE BLOOD COVENANT	2.50	
	WHAT TO DO WHEN NOTHING SEEMS TO WORK*	.75	
	WHAT TO DO WHEN THE TEMPTER COMES	1.25	
	YOU CAN CHANGE YOUR DESTINY	1.50	

*AVAILABLE IN SPANISH

SUBTOTAL A	
SUBTOTAL B	
POSTAGE & HANDLING	$1.00
TOTAL AMOUNT ENCLOSED	

NAME _____

ADDRESS _____

CITY _____ STATE _____ ZIP _____

WRITE FOR A COMPLETE LIST OF JOHN OSTEEN'S TEACHING MATERIALS IN THE JOHN OSTEEN FAITH LIBRARY CATALOGUE. MANNA MAGAZINE IS AVAILABLE UPON REQUEST FREE AND POSTAGE PAID. WRITE TO:

JOHN OSTEEN MINISTRIES
P.O. BOX 23117
HOUSTON, TEXAS 77228